He doesn't need to play the roulette. He needs to find the doing, that enlights his spirit. Nor does she crave the bottle. She merely seeks to be. One moment. One lifetime. Craving is the lesser alternative for one who isn't yet. Hasn't become. It can take a thousand spins, a thousand bottles to understand. To accept the calling. Of your soul. Of the universe. Speaking. Louder and louder. Through the spins. Through the bottles. Saying, wake up. To wake up. To wake up

The Gambling Addiction Journal

Copyright © 2018- C.W. V. Straaten
Published by: True Potential Project

ISBN: 9781791562403

All rights reserved.

Disclaimer

This book is not intended to be a substitute for medical advice or treatment. Any person with a condition requiring medical attention should consult a qualified medical practitioner or suitable therapist.

The information provided in this book is stated to be truthful and consistent, in that any liability, in terms of inattention or otherwise, by any usage or abuse of any policies, processes, or directions contained within is the solitary and utter responsibility of the recipient reader. Under no circumstances will any legal responsibility or blame be held against the publisher for any reparation, damages, or monetary loss due to the information herein, either directly or indirectly.

The Gambling Addiction Journal

A 90-Day Recovery Guide

Created by:
C.W. V. STRAATEN

Instagram: become_recovery

A Message From The Author

In Leo Tolstoy's acclaimed novel *The Death of Ivan Illich* one of the main character is contemplating the following question on his deathbed,

"What if my whole life has been wrong?"

Why do we wait to live the life we're meant to be? To fulfill our calling. The present doesn't have to be a continuation of the past.

There is the beauty of a new beginning, every day, each moment.

Don't wait on your deathbed, it isn't worth the risk.

Introduction

Recovery
/rɪˈkʌv.ɚ.i/

noun

The process of becoming successful or normal again after problems.

If you read this text, you know there is a problem. That one habit is taken over. That this particular habit is slowly becoming who you are. A dark intruder that controls every area of your life. Not in the last place, personal relationships, finances and your self-esteem. Gambling is a risky endeavor. A game that could lure you in and crush you into a dark pit of loneliness and chasing.

However, it is crucial to state that although it's tremendous powers, gambling can never control totally who you are and what you do. There always is a tiny piece within you that recognizes this. A glimpse of hope in a pile of dust. Deep down you know you can choose. You know you can open the door to a new life. That believe, that inevitable fact, gives you the direction to control your problems. To cure your addiction and find out what it really is you're trying to numb. Choose the right way. This moment always has the life-changing opportunity to change. To choose a different decision that leads to a new life.

This 90-Day journal is created to guide you on your way to a new life. I have been addicted to gambling for many years of my life. I know the dark powers of gambling and of addiction. And above all I know that it is possible to take the opposite direction. To go on a road of recovery. This journal will first and foremost create a new and hopeful sense of awareness. It lures your addiction out of the dark places of your unconsciousness and in to the light of your waking consciousness. There it is in *your* power.

With the guidance of this journal you will recognize the patterns that lead to gambling, how you can prevent it from happening again and how you can recover fast from a relapse. Furthermore the questions in this journal will set you on a road of self-discovery that covers way more than just your addiction. Recovery in this sense equals transformation. Into living the life you're supposed to lived.

The Gambling Addiction Journal provides a new and different question each day. Furthermore I've added inspiring notes of my own recovery journey throughout the book. Lastly, this journal is full with inspirational and uplifting quotes, to start your day right and help you to answer the questions truthfully. You could use this journal as a simple and empowering guide during your recovery. The integration of a short daily journaling habit is sometimes worth the investment alone. I carefully created the question and pieces of advice to give you the best experience over a three-month period. My advice is to dedicate five to ten minutes a day to this journal. Make it a certain positive habit, that is sure to improve yourself every single day.

I wish you courage and faith on your recovery journey; this moment is as good as any to make a new beginning. Take the opposite direction and start living.

C.W. V. Straaten, The Netherlands 2018

How To Use This Journal

On every page, you'll find a new day, and a different question. There is enough space on each page to answer the question and do some more journaling. If you want more journaling space, there are a couple of blank, lined pages at the end of this journal. There is a specific order in these questions, to give you the best benefit over three months. I recommend setting a particular time each day for your journaling exercises; for example during your morning routine, or before you go to bed. Some topics in this journal will keep returning, such as recognizing your own strengths and gratefulness. I did this, because I believe that these components are fundamental when you want to stay on your recovery journey and create a life-changing effect.

"It is never too late to be what you might have been."

George Eliot

Daily Recovery Inspirations

If you want to focus on becoming free from addiction
& commit to recovery every day, follow my instagram account.
With a recovery inspiration every day.

Instagram: become_recovery
https://www.instagram.com/become_recovery/.

Or you can search on C.W. V. Straaten.

Day 1

"Happiness is not something ready made. It comes from your own actions."

Dalai Lama XIV

If you would use the amazing need to gamble for something constructive in your life, what could you accomplish in the next three months?

And within one year?

Day 2

So what other can a man attract who is craving every minute of the day, than a reality where he just can't get. He jumps, and jumps, only sometimes hitting his target, but when he jumps again, the target is higher, and higher.

What precisely have you always loved about gambling?

Day 3

"But to be angry at myself or at my addiction isn't the right way.
Understanding my addictive behavior has given me peace.
It wasn't the drinking that was the core problem,
it was the pain that I needed to numb."

Joanne Edmund, *The Sobriety Journal*

What part of you needs recovery from gambling the most?

Day 4

"If you can change your mind, you can change your life."

William James

What part of you is craving gambling the most?

Day 5

After years of gambling I found out that gambling equalled: losing money, losing time, loneliness and destruction. These became such fundamental beliefs that overtime my craving for gambling disappeared altogether.

What statements could you make about gambling after months/years of gambling problems?

Day 6

Then to stop the jumping. To liberate from the eternal craving, one has to be aware of the craving. One has to know that craving attracts only more craving. For what monster is really so scary in the lamplight of strength, determination and love?

Imagine you would be on a recovery road for the next three months, how would your life look like 90 days from now?

Day 7

Small steps have the incredible power to become big changes. Both destructive and constructive (positive). I frequently ask myself. "What is one thing I can do today to make this day worthwhile?". It's a simple question, but the benefits are hard to exaggerate

What is one thing you could do this week,
to improve your recovery journey?
Make the commitment to follow through.

Day 8

"I am but a small pencil in the hand of a writing God."

Mother Teresa

What does recovery mean to you?

Day 9

"It takes a very long time to become young."

Pablo Picasso

Is the person who first decided to gamble, still the same person today?

Day 10

"Hope is the thing with feathers
That perches in the soul
And sings the tune without the words
And never stops at all."

Emily Dickinson

Which of your core beliefs don't improve your life?

Day 11

So tell me then, to what man,
to what women is the reality of addiction attracted?
For it was said, that what you think you become.
And the wiser man knows that you attract what you become.

What advice would you give to someone who is about to relapse gambling?

Day 12

"I am not afraid of storms, for I am learning how to sail my ship."

Louisa May Alcott

What has been the influence of your gambling problem on your past?

Day 13

"Hide not your talents, they for use were made,
What's a sundial in the shade?"

Benjamin Franklin

If you could imagine a future without gambling,
how would that future look like?

Day 14

Certain energies attract certain realities. Like attracts like.
As the clean streets in a good neighborhood,
and the dirty streets in a bad neighbourhood.
Not a question of what comes first, but a continuous cycle.
Where everything is connected.
No first, no second.
No second, no first.

Describe yourself during a gambling binge,
totally destructive and unstoppable.

Day 15

"You will not be punished for your anger;
you will be punished by your anger."

Siddhārtha Gautama

Who does inspire you?

Day 16

Awareness in itself is a powerful source to solve a problem. Once you recognize what gambling actually does to your life, by seeing the financial numbers and tracking your gambling time, it will be easier to cease such a destructive habit altogether.

How much money have you lost gambling in the past 6 months? Try to make an accurate investigation, by going over bank statements. Or, if it is too tough, make a rough estimation

Day 17

"The unexamined life is not worth living."

Socrates

How has gambling been a strategy to escape tough situations?

Day 18

Habits always have a cue. A starting signal. Sometimes several steps are needed to 'execute' the habit. Be an investigator and understand your gambling habit. What exactly leads you to gambling?

What exactly is the pattern in your life that leads to gambling?

See for more information about how a habit works the following article: https://charlesduhigg.com/how-habits-work/

Day 19

"What is that you express in your eyes?
It seems to me more than all the print I have read in my life."

Walt Whitman

Write down seven things you are grateful for in your life.

Day 20

It's not the craving who can heal the craving.
As it isn't the worry who can stop worrying.

Write down three small things you could do to make your life easier.

Day 21

"The best portion of a good man's life:
his little, nameless unremembered acts of kindness and love."

William Wordsworth

Look at your list from yesterday.
Pick one of them and make the commitment to yourself to integrate it in your life immediately. Write down how you are going to integrate it, so that from this day forward you will make your life at least a little bit easier.

Day 22

"Far better it is to dare mighty things, to win glorious triumphs, even though checkered by failure, than to take rank with those poor spirits who neither enjoy much nor suffer much, because they live in the gray twilight that knows neither victory nor defeat."

Theodore Roosevelt

If you felt safe enough to be who you really are, would there be gambling in your life?

Day 23

"Be thine own palace, or the world's thy jail."

John Donne

What is your go-to strategy for dealing with rejection?

Day 24

"Remember that sometimes not getting what you want
is a wonderful stroke of luck."

Dalai Lama XIV

Once again investigate your gambling habit.
What is one thing you could do, to easily dismantle the pattern
that leads to gamble.

Day 25

It is tough to take a good look at your own life, certainly when life is clouded by addiction. In self-reflection, however, lies the astounding power to lasting change. How could we change ourselves, if we don't know what is beneath the surface?

Is there a correlation between your level of self-confidence and your gambling problem?

Day 26

"Let us be grateful to the people who make us happy;
they are the charming gardeners who make our souls blossom."

Marcel Proust

Write down three things that make your life worthwhile.

Day 27

*It is not that addiction doesn't serve a purpose. Quite the contrary. It is like an alarm bell, trying to wake you up: "Hey, something needs attention!" There are valuable lessons addiction can teach us.
You just got to be aware of it.*

What has your gambling problem taught you about yourself?

Day 28

"We judge ourselves by what we feel capable of doing, while others judge us by what we have already done."

Henry Wadsworth Longfellow

Write down three things you could do to prevent a relapse.

Day 29

Relapses do happen. For almost all of us, it's part of recovery. And it is not the end of the world. What matters is how you deal with it. It is simply a signal that you still have work to do on your recovery journey. Maybe you have to tweak your approach here and there. First and foremost you have to think about how you deal with it, when a relapse occurs. Preparation is gold. You will thank yourself for it later.

Write down three things you could do to recover from a relapse.

Day 30

"In character, in manner, in style, in all the things,
the supreme excellence is simplicity."

Henry Wadsworth Longfellow

If you would continue to gamble, how would your life look like in one year? And in five years?

Day 31

It can take a thousand spins, a thousand bets to understand.
To accept the calling. Of your soul. Of the universe.
Speaking. Louder and louder. Through the spins. Through the bottles.
Saying, wake up. To wake up. To wake up.

What could you do to be your own best friend?

Day 32

"Forever is composed of nows."

Emily Dickinson

What is the one piece of advice you would give to other people with a gambling problem?

Day 33

"If we had no winter, the spring would not be so pleasant: if we did not sometimes taste of adversity, prosperity would not be so welcome."

Anne Bradstreet

What is something you are passionate about,
that because of gambling didn't get the attention it needed?

Day 34

"Come friends, it's not too late to seek a newer world."

Alfred Lord Tennyson

How could being more grateful, improve your recovery journey?

Day 35

"One ought, every day at least, to hear a little song, read a good poem, see a fine picture, and, if it were possible, to speak a few reasonable words."

Johann Wolfgang von Goethe

Write down three things that make you feel grateful about last week

Day 36

The awful thing about gambling, among others, is that it could potentially ruin your financial situation. I had horrendous debt, but managed to work my way out of it. First of all to cut expenses and make honest appointments with my creditors. Secondly, to create extra income. There were moments I felt that I would never climb out of the financial mud. But small constructive steps taken consistently + time...
Produces life-changing results.

What is one small thing you could do this week
to improve your financial situation?

Day 37

"What is now proved was once only imagined."

William Blake

What purpose did gambling serve in your life?

Day 38

"Knowing yourself is the beginning of all wisdom."

Aristotle

What is one thing about yourself you would gladly share with the world?

Day 39

"The imagination is not a state: it is the human existence itself."

William Blake

Imagine, you would go to a psychologist today,
what three pieces of advice would he or she give to you?

Day 40

"He who is best prepared can best serve his moment of inspiration."

Samuel Taylor Coleridge

What does scare you about your gambling addiction?

Day 41

Most of the time you just fear monsters under the bed. And the truth is... there are no monsters under the bed. But, if there are, it is most likely that you will find a way to deal with them.

Look at yesterday's answer.

Is your fear really based in reality?
If so, how could you prepare for the worst?

Day 42

"Life is not a having and a getting, but a being and a becoming."

Matthew Arnold

Write down three achievements that make you feel proud about yourself.

Day 43

"Resolve to be thyself;
and know, that he who finds himself,
loses his misery."

Matthew Arnold

Why is it a waste of time if you would continue to gamble?

Day 44

I've listened countless times to the same YouTube videos about overcoming gambling addiction. Even during my sleep. I've written down statements about recovery and the horrors of gambling addiction on post it's in my apartment. Yes, affirmations do work. Just not on their own, your actions should carry your affirmations.

What is one affirmation you could repeat to yourself over and over again to knock out gambling for good?

Day 45

"Always laugh when you can, it is cheap medicine."

Lord Byron

What talent you have will easily create you a positive income stream that will beat the gambling debts?

Day 46

"It had long since come to my attention that people of accomplishment rarely sat back and let things happen to them.
They went out and happened to things."

Leonardo da Vinci

Look at yesterday's answer.
What are three things you could do to improve your unique talent?

Day 47

"I have absolutely no pleasure in the stimulants in which I sometimes so madly indulge. It has not been in the pursuit of pleasure that I have periled life and reputation and reason. It has been the desperate attempt to escape from torturing memories, from a sense of insupportable loneliness and a dread of some strange impending doom."

Edgar Allan Poe

What would you like people to understand about addiction?

Day 48

"I am the master of my fate:
I am the captain of my soul."

William Ernest Henley

Do you believe you are a victim of addiction?
Why or why not?

Day 49

"The art of being wise is knowing what to overlook."

William James

Look at yourself in the mirror for at least three minutes straight.
Set an alarm. What do you see?

Day 50

Life reflects the person who is looking at her.
When you look at life, know that she stares back.
Who you are, is what you see.

Which quality/talent did your gambling addiction ruin the most?

Day 51

"Begin, be bold, and venture to be wise."

Horace

Name seven positive character traits about yourself.

Day 52

Don't be fooled that all you want is to quit gambling. If you've ever chosen to gamble, up to a destructive point, there is a part of you that wants it. In consequence it becomes scary to quit altogether. The question remains, what do you 'lose' by quitting gambling?

Something inside you always 've wanted to gamble.
So what makes you afraid to forever stop gambling?

Day 53

"The greatest weapon against stress
is our ability to choose one thought over another."

William James

What is one small thing you could do on a daily basis
to stay on your recovery journey?

Day 54

Inspiration could be seeked. Through books, articles, YouTube videos, friendships, and so on. Find out what inspires you and integrate it in your life. Create a healthy ecosystem where you could flourish.

What inspires you?

Day 55

"What lies behind us and what lies before us
are tiny matters compared to what lies within us."

Ralph Waldo Emerson

How could you begin to forgive yourself for the destruction your gambling addiction caused?

Day 56

"If you want to be happy, be."

Leo Tolstoy

Are you still blaming people for how your life turned out to be? Why or why not?

Day 57

Change seems to come real slow. Until one day you wake up and realize life is different. Not because of that very day, but of all the work you've put in before. It was difficult for me to realize this in the beginning months of my recovery. I wanted changes, in fact I needed changes fast. At least that's what I thought. But why question Life? If you feel you're on the right path, have faith in yourself. Have faith in life, The Universe. You'll end up where you need to be.

What subtle changes have you noticed about yourself over the past few months

Day 58

"To live is the rarest thing in the world. Most people exist, that is all."

Oscar Wilde

What is one small thing you could do to make today worthwhile?

Day 59

"Every trail has its end, and every calamity brings its lesson!"

James Fenimore Cooper

How is your life influenced by worries, negative thoughts and anxieties?

Day 60

Stop trying to change the mirror.
Out there nothing brings fulfillment.
All what's brought to you is a mere reflection.
It's life bouncing back.
The thoughts.
The being.

How much time do you spend each day
getting to know yourself better?

Day 61

"Happiness is like a butterfly which, when pursued, is always beyond our grasp, but, if you will sit down quietly, may alight upon you."

Nathaniel Hawthorne

Write down all the things you missed out on because of your gambling habit.

Day 62

An important but difficult question I've asked myself repeatedly during my recovery is, "What will I sacrifice if I continue gambling?" The answer never satisfied me. The time, effort and money wasted for a superficial, destructive gambling habit. All these things, time, effort and money are precious. Definitely time, the most valuable of all. Thus the question remains, do you want to spend your time gambling?

Is gambling your purpose here on earth?

What do you sacrifice if you continue to gamble?

Day 63

"Love is never lost. If not reciprocated,
it will flow back and soften and purify the heart."

Washington Irving

What is one small thing you could do this week to improve your financial situation? And what is one thing you could do *right now* to improve your financial situation? Write it down. Then, don't wait, take action.

Day 64

What once was a winter is now the time to rest and reflect.
What once was the reason for sorrow, now is an element of flow.

Where in your life are you too hard for yourself?

Day 65

It is the love for life, the love for yourself that brought you here.
And whenever the hardship comes in,
the shadow falls, know that, always accessible is that sparkle of light,
even shining just a little bit, can be enough to break through,
to change, to take a turn for the better.

What anger is waiting to be expressed for a long time now?

Day 66

The question I got some time from people, is, "Are you never afraid your addiction will return?" And it is a fair question. A thought that is in the back of the mind of most recovered addicts. First, I believe you have to stop identifying yourself as 'an addict' or 'a recovered addict'. For the purpose of clarity, we're using 'recovered addict' or 'former gambler' to advertise my books. But in reality I don't identify myself as a 'recovered addict', but just as a person. As me. And as 'me' there are a thousand things that can happen. I have influence on the course of my life, but far less than I like to believe. I am not afraid that my addiction will return. I know that my intention is right and life will always give me exactly what I need. And winters are a normal part of life.

Do you believe addiction could be conquered? Why or why not?

Day 67

The time, energy and thinking someone wastes on addictive behaviour; what if one uses that for something else? Can it be that on some level an addict develops his or her creativity enormously because of the elaborate ways one uses to continue the addiction? And if that's right, what are the amazing creative possibilities for one who "conquers" his or hers addiction?

Are their people in your life who actually
draw you to destructive behaviour?

Day 68

"Watch and pray, dear, never get tired of trying, and never think it is impossible to conquer your fault."

Louisa May Alcott

What lessons could people in recovery learn from you?

Day 69

"It is better to fail in originality than to succeed in imitation."

Herman Melville

Is the way you are communicating with yourself empowering or disempowering to your life?

Day 70

When you don't stop a pattern intentionally, any pattern, it will go bigger overtime. It starts to become a rhythm. Hard to escape. Mind you, this works both ways: negatively and positively. Pattern recognition is therefore one of the secrets to live a much, much more successful life. Whatever success means to you.

What worries have the most devastating effect on your life?

Day 71

*If you closely examine your worries, you'll see that they're mere thoughts.
And sometimes accompanied by emotions, sensations in the body. Sit down
for a moment and pay attention to what worries actually are.
Become aware of what has such a gripping
and disempowering effect on our lives.*

Look at yesterday's answer.

Are these worries based in reality?
If so, how could you prepare yourself for the worst case scenario?

Day 72

"A path is made by walking on it."

Zhuang Zhou

What is one thing you could do this week, to improve your relationship with yourself?

Day 73

"You'll never find a rainbow if you're looking down"

Charlie Chaplin

What three qualities make you stand out from other people?

Day 74

"He who has a why to live for can bear almost any how."

Friedrich Nietzsche

What is your biggest "Why" for the things you do?

Day 75

"I am a part of all that I have met."

Alfred Tennyson

What is the one compliment you need right now?

Day 76

There is a magic power in giving. Wholeheartedly giving, without expecting something in return. During my gambling years and the first period of my recovery I had periods where I had an intense feeling of loneliness. An endless black pit. One day I decided, instead of waiting in my apartment with the curtains closed, to give what I wanted myself: connection, inspiration, love. Eventually it came back tenfold.

How could you give that, what you so desperately need,
to other people, without expecting something in return?

Day 77

"A man with outward courage dares to die;
a man with inner courage dares to live."

Lao Tzu

What leads your life, your intuition or your mind?

Day 78

"It is not down on any map; true places never are."

Herman Melville

What is your definition of an addiction?

Day 79

"Never to suffer would never to have been blessed."

Edgar Allan Poe

What is one thing you could do each morning
to start the day with the right mindset?

Day 80

"If you have built castles in the air, your work need not be lost; that is where they should be. Now put the foundations under them."

Henry David Thoreau

What constructive habits empower your life right now?
Could you add one more (small) constructive habit in your life?

Day 81

"We first make our habits, then our habits make us."

John Dryden

Look at yesterday's answer.
How could you integrate this new constructive habit in your life?

Day 82

It's amazing how many lessons you've actually learned in your life. How many times you've picked yourself up. The values of these lessons are often not seen. Try to look at your past as an ocean of knowledge, waiting to be used.

Write down one past experience when you overcame 'failure'.

Day 83

"I have not failed. I've just found 10,000 ways that won't work."

Thomas A. Edison

Look at yesterday's answer.
How could this experience help you in the future?

Day 84

"When you arise in the morning think of what a privilege it is to be alive, to think, to enjoy, to love ..."

Marcus Aurelius

Imagine you would meet your addiction today,
what would you tell it?

Day 85

Being aware, or living in a state of mindfulness, is a continuous state. It is a choice to shine the light on 'everything'. Your own life, suppressed emotions, thoughts, your mind and the world around you. It is a freeing state of living, where you face your fears and give yourself the opportunity to truly live the life you want to live.

Where in your life do you still recognize patterns of your addiction?

Day 86

"Do not spoil what you have by desiring what you have not; remember that what you now have was once among the things you only hoped for."

Epicurus

What makes you feel grateful about yesterday?

Day 87

By numbing the pain it only comes back bigger.

If courageously dealing with an addiction is a superpower, what else could you do with this superpower?

Day 88

"Courage is the first of human qualities
because it is the quality which guarantees the others."

Aristotle

What would happen if you acted as your most courageous self
when it comes to making choices in the next coming month?

Day 89

It is hard to exaggerate what could happen once you know you're on the right path. It takes action, uncomfortable conversations, rigorous self-reflection and awareness. But glimpses of light make it all worth. Because it is not about the future. It's never about the future. It is happening now. You can make the right choice each moment. Literally every moment. Because this moment, the 'right now' is all that we have. When you do what is right, the moment changes. Your life changes.

Imagine you would stay on this recovery road for the next three months, how would your life look like 90 days from now?

Day 90

You will start noticing that when you move away from addiction,
that different thoughts will arrive.
And after an initial period of changing thoughts,
your words will reflect these thoughts.
Eventually actions follow as well.

After three months of journaling what have you learned
about your gambling problems and recovery?

About The Author

C.W. V. Straaten is the author of *The Addiction Recovery Workbook* and *The Gambling Addiction Workbook*. After living in several countries, the author now resides in Buenos Aires, Argentina, working on his inspiring self-help guides and a new novel. In the fall of 2018 his new self-help book '*The Addiction Recovery Journal*' was released on Amazon.

Through his unique self-help book for recovery, The Gambling Addiction Workbook, he has helped many in understanding and overcoming their gambling addiction. His new book The Addiction Recovery Workbook, where he wrote his inspiring masterplan to help addicts around the world to conquer their addiction, was released in January 2018.

C.W. V. Straaten struggled himself with the hypnotic demons of addiction until he finally discovered how to free himself of his addictive behavior. Now he has been more than 4 years recovered and is dedicating his life to writing and publishing books.

Did you like this journal? You could help spread the word for this book, to take a few seconds and leave a review or rating on Amazon and/or Goodreads. It means a lot.

For Daily Recovery Inspirations follow me on Instagram,
Instagram: become_recovery

Personal Journal

The Gambling Addiction Journal

Made in United States
Troutdale, OR
02/20/2025